A Humanist Wedding Service

A Humanist Wedding Service

Corliss Lamont

Prometheus Books

59 John Glenn Drive
Amherst, New York 14228-2119

Published by Prometheus Books

Inquiries should be addressed to
Prometheus Books
59 John Glenn Drive
Amherst, New York 14228–2119
VOICE: 716–691–0133, ext. 210
FAX: 716–691–0137
WWW.PROMETHEUSBOOKS.COM

ISBN: 978-0-87975-000-8

Printed in the United States of America on acid-free paper

Acknowledgments

Voices, Summer 1945, for Arthur Davison Ficke's "Sonnet."

A Humanist Wedding Service

The couple has been assigned names in order to avoid the awkwardness of blank spaces. The Reader may be a church official, a Humanist Counselor, a Justice of the Peace, a family friend, or anyone whom the couple selects.

Reader: *Pat* and *Chris* have come to love each other deeply and sincerely. They now wish to unite their lives and establish a home together. In this ceremony they dedicate themselves to the happiness and well-being of each other.

Marriage is a supreme sharing of experience and

an adventure in the most intimate of human relationships. It is the joyous uniting of two people whose comradeship and mutual understanding have flowered into romance. Today *Pat* and *Chris* proclaim their love to the world, and we who are gathered here rejoice *with* them and *for* them in the new life they now undertake together.

This wedding in the Humanist spirit celebrates the joy and the beauty of life. Humanism sees an individual as an active and inseparable unity of body and personality. Reason is the guide, but reason never separate from the emotions and strivings of the whole person; so that emotion and intellect functioning together provide the firmest foundation for married love.

The blessed warmth of love permeates one's entire being: When two people "are successfully in love, their whole activity is energized and victorious. They walk better, their digestion improves, they think more clearly, their secret worries drop away, the world is fresh and interesting, and they can do more than they dreamed they could do. In love of this kind sexual intimacy is not the dead end of desire but periodic affirmation of the inward delight pervading an active life. Love of this sort can grow; it is not, like youth, a moment that comes and is gone, remaining only a memory of something which cannot be recovered. It can grow because it has something to grow upon and grow with. It does not become contracted and stale, because it has for its object all the objects with which the two lovers are concerned. Love endures only when the lovers love many things together, and not merely each other."*

Pat and *Chris* hold in common the interests and ideals of a Humanist world. Living together in this way, they will deepen their love for each other. The transfiguring power of that love will reach out in compassionate concern for their fellow Humanists, indeed to the whole community of humankind.

---

*Walter Lippmann, *A Preface to Morals*, Macmillan, 1929, pp. 296, 308.

It is a Humanist belief that there should be equality among people in every relevant way, and that it is especially important for this principle to be recognized in the marriage relationship. Humanists repudiate the old tradition of one partner who meekly obeys the other. Marriage must be a cooperative venture in every sense. It is a relationship based on love, respect, and a determination on the part of both partners to adjust to each other's temperaments and moods—in health or sickness, joy or sadness, ease or hardship.

The marriage of *Pat* and *Chris* means the creation of a new home and a new family. The family has continued to show great hardihood as an institution and thrives throughout the world. In an age when many traditional values have crumbled, it becomes all the more important to recognize the significance of devoted and affectionate family life. We therefore welcome *Pat* and *Chris* to the great community of married folk.

It is time to turn to what the poets say about love. And, first, there is this Lover's Chant for *Pat* and *Chris*:

Possess me forever
    O sweet delirium!
Sweep through my restless blood
    O delicious fever!
Intoxicate my mind
    O surging madness!
Fill utterly my being
    O mystic joy!
And spur me to great deeds
    O soul's ferment!

We know that *Pat* and *Chris* are going to spur each other on to the greatest possible deeds on behalf of peace, freedom, and a truly Humanist society.

The legal part of the ceremony which follows must be performed by a duly qualified official. The couple stands.

Official: *Chris*, will you have *Pat* to be your wedded spouse, to share your life, and do you pledge that you will love, honor, and tenderly care for her [him] in all the varying circumstances of your lives?

Chris: I will.

Official: *Pat*, will you have *Chris* to be your wedded spouse, to share your life, and do you pledge that you will love, honor, and care for him [her] in tenderness and affection through all the varying experiences of your lives?

Pat: I will.

If a bride is to be given away, these two lines may be used:

Official: Who gives this woman to be married here today?

Family representative: I, her father.

The couple then addresses each other:

Chris: *Pat,* I acknowledge my love and respect for you and invite you to share my life as I hope to share yours. I promise always to be conscious of your development as well as my own. I shall seek through kindness and understanding to achieve with you the life we have envisioned. *If a ring is to be given, add:* In token of my love and devotion, I place this ring on your finger.

Pat: *Chris,* I acknowledge my love and respect for you and invite you to share my life as I hope to share yours. I promise always to recognize you as an equal individual, and always to be conscious of your development as well as my own. I shall seek through kindness and understanding to achieve with you the life we have envisioned. *If a ring is to be given, add:* In token of my love and devotion, I place this ring on your finger.

Official: Inasmuch as *Pat* and *Chris* have consented together in this ceremony to live in wedlock and have witnessed their vows in the presence of this company *by the giving and receiving of rings*, I now pronounce by the authority invested in me and in accordance with the laws of the State of _____ that they are married.

Reader: As a blessing for *Pat* and *Chris*, we read these lines from a Native American ceremony:

> Now you will feel no rain, for each of you
>   will be shelter for the other.

> Now you will feel no cold, for each of you
>   will be warmth to the other.

> Now there is no more loneliness.

> Now you are two persons, but there is only
>   one life before you.

Go now to your dwelling to enter into
    the days of your life together.

And may your days be good, and long
    upon the earth.

Before our toast to *Pat* and *Chris*, we will all sing
Ben Jonson's love song "Drink to Me Only with
Thine Eyes" to the old familiar tune:

Drink to me only with thine eyes
And I will pledge with mine;
Or leave a kiss but in the cup,
And I'll not ask for wine.
The thirst that from the soul doth rise
Doth ask a drink divine,
But might I of Jove's nectar sup,
I would not change for thine.

*Each couple may wish to include other songs or music at
this point in the service.*

The Reader now takes up a bowl of red wine provided by the couple's families or friends and proposes a toast:

Reader: On behalf of all who are here today and all who are friends of this radiant couple, I drink to long life and happiness for *Pat* and *Chris*.

The years of our lives are as a cup of wine poured out for us to drink. May the cup of your lives, *Pat* and *Chris*, be sweet and full. Drink now to each other from this bowl and so give the final consecration to your marriage.

Pat and Chris drink to each other.

ADDITIONAL SUGGESTIONS
FOR POETRY

The poems below may be substituted for or used in addition to those included in the service. The couple may wish to read aloud a poem during the ceremony.

From *Heritage*

What fills the heart of man
Is not that his life must fade,
But that out of his dark there can
A light like a rose be made,

That seeing a snow-flake fall
His heart is lifted up,
That hearing a meadow-lark call
For a moment he will stop
To rejoice in the musical air
To delight in the fertile earth
And the flourishing everywhere
Of spring and spring's rebirth.
And never a woman or man
Walked through their quickening hours
But found for some brief span
An intervale of flowers,
Where love for a man or a woman
So captured the heart's beat
That they and all things human
Danced on rapturous feet.

THEODORE SPENCER

Sonnet CXVI

Let me not to the marriage of true minds
Admit impediments. Love is not love
Which alters when it alteration finds,
Or bends with the remover to remove:
Oh no! it is an ever-fixed mark,
That looks on tempests and is never shaken;
It is the star to every wandering bark,
Whose worth's unknown, although his
    height be taken.
Love's not Time's fool, though rosy lips and
    cheeks
Within his bending sickle's compass come;
Love alters not with his brief hours and
    weeks,
But bears it out even to the edge of doom.
If this be error, and upon me prov'd,
I never writ, nor no man ever lov'd.

WILLIAM SHAKESPEARE

Sonnet XXIX

When, in disgrace with fortune and men's
  eyes,
I all alone beweep my outcast state,
And trouble deaf heaven with my bootless
  cries,
And look upon myself and curse my fate,
Wishing me like to one more rich in hope,
Featur'd like him, like him with friends
  possess'd,
Desiring this man's art and that man's scope,
With what I most enjoy contented least;
Yet in these thoughts myself almost
  despising,
Haply I think on thee—and then my state,
Like to the lark at break of day arising
From sullen earth, sings hymns at heaven's
  gate;

For thy sweet love remember'd such wealth
    brings
That then I scorn to change my state with
    kings.

WILLIAM SHAKESPEARE

Sonnet XCI

Some glory in their birth, some in their skill,
Some in their wealth, some in their body's force;
Some in their garments, though new-fangled
    ill;
Some in their hawks and hounds, some in
    their horse;
And every humour hath his adjunct pleasure,
Wherein it finds a joy above the rest;
But these particulars are not my measure;
All these I better in one general best.
Thy love is better than high birth to me,
Richer than wealth, prouder than garments'
    cost
Of more delight than hawks or horses be;
And having thee, of all men's pride I boast;
Wretched in this alone, that thou mayst take
All this away, and me most wretched make.

WILLIAM SHAKESPEARE

The Passionate Shepherd to His Love

Come live with me and be my Love
And we will all the pleasures prove
That hills and valleys, dales and fields,
Or woods or steepy mountain yields.

And we will sit upon the rocks,
And see the shepherds feed their flocks
By shallow rivers, to whose falls
Melodious birds sing madrigals.

And I will make thee beds of roses
And a thousand fragrant posies;
A cap of flowers, and a kirtle
Embroider'd all with leaves of myrtle.

A gown made of the finest wool
Which from our pretty lambs we pull;
Fur-lined slippers for the cold,
With buckles of the purest gold.

A belt of straw and ivy-buds
With coral clasps and amber studs;
And if these pleasures may thee move,
Come live with me and be my Love.

The shepherd swains shall dance and sing
For thy delight each May morning;
If these delights thy mind may move,
Then live with me and be my Love.

CHRISTOPHER MARLOWE

Sonnet

Love is the simplest of all earthly things.
It needs no grandeur of celestial trust
In more than what it is, no holy wings:
It stands with honest feet in honest dust,
And is the body's blossoming in clear air
Of trustfulness and joyance when alone
Two mortals pass beyond the hour's despair
And claim that Paradise which is their own.
Amid a universe of sweat and blood,
Beyond the glooms of all the nation's hate,
Lovers, forgetful of the poisoned mood
Of the loud world, in secret ere too late
A gentle sacrament may celebrate
Before their private altar of the good.

ARTHUR DAVISON FICKE

Love-Song

How can I hinder or restrain my soul
So that it does not yearn for yours? And how
Can it be lured to life apart from you?
Gladly would I (had I complete control)
Transport it, a dark secret thing, to new
And untried depths of silence. But I know
How everything that stirs me, stirs you too;
How you and I are like a bow that's bound,
Though with two strings, to give a single
    sound.
Upon what instrument have we been
    spanned?
And what strange player plays us, heart and
    hand?
O long, sweet song!

RAINER MARIA RILKE
(Translated by Louis Untermeyer)

From *Paradise Lost*

With thee conversing I forget all time,
All seasons and their change, all please alike.
Sweet is the breath of morn, her rising
    sweet,
With charm of earliest birds; pleasant the
    sun
When first on this delightful land he spreads
His orient beams on herb, tree, fruit, and
    flowr,
Glist'ring with dew; fragrant the fertile earth
After soft showers; and sweet the coming on
Of grateful ev'ning mild; then silent night
With this her solemn bird and this fair moon
And these the gems of heav'n her starry
    train:
But neither breath of morn when she ascends
With charm of earliest birds, nor rising sun
On this delightful land, nor herb, fruit, flowr,

Glist'ring with dew, nor fragrance after
    showers,
Nor grateful ev'ning mild, nor silent night
With this her solemn bird, nor walk by
    moon
Or glittering star-light without thee is sweet.

JOHN MILTON

To Lesbia

My Lesbia, let us love and live
And to the winds, my Lesbia, give
Each cold restraint, each boding fear
Of age and all her saws severe.
Yon sun now posting to the main
Will set,—but 'tis to rise again;
But we, when once our mortal light
Is set, must sleep in endless night.
Then come, with whom alone I'll live,
A thousand kisses take and give!
Another thousand!—to the store
Add hundreds—then a thousand more!
And when they to a million mount,
Let confusion take the account,—
That you, the number never knowing,
May continue still bestowing—

That I for joys may never pine
Which never can again be mine!

CATULLUS
(Translated by Samuel T. Coleridge)

From *The Prophet*

You were born together, and together you
    shall be forevermore.
You shall be together when the white wings
    of death scatter your days.
But let there be spaces in your togetherness,
And let the winds of the heavens dance
    between you.
Love one another, but make not a bond of
    love:
Let it rather be a moving sea between the
    shores of your souls.
Fill each other's cup but drink not from one
    cup.
Give one another of your bread but eat not
    from the same loaf.
Sing and dance together and be joyous,
    but let each one of you be alone,

Even as the strings of a lute are alone
    though they quiver with the same music.
Give your hearts, but not into each other's
    keeping.
For only the hand of Life can contain your
    hearts.
And stand together yet not too near
    together:
For the pillars of the temple stand apart,
And the oak tree and the cypress grow not in
    each other's shadow.

KAHLIL GIBRAN

From *Song of Solomon*, Chapter IV

Behold, thou art fair, my love; behold, thou
    art fair;
Thou hast doves' eyes within thy locks:
Thy hair is as a flock of goats,
That appear from Mount Gilead.

Thy teeth are like a flock of ewes that are
    newly shorn,
Which are come up from the washing:
Whereof every one hath twins,
And none is barren among them.

Thy lips are like a thread of scarlet,
And thy speech is comely:
Thy temples are like a piece of pomegranate
Within thy locks.
Thy neck is like the tower of David builded
    for an armoury,
Whereon there hang a thousand bucklers,

All shields of mighty men.
Thy two breasts are like two young roes that
    are twins,
Which feed among the lilies.

Until the day break, and the shadows flee
    away,
I will get me to the mountain of myrrh
And to the hill of frankincense.

Thou are all fair, my love:
And there is no spot in thee,
Come with me from Lebanon, my bride,
With me from Lebanon.
Look from the top of Amana,
From the top of Senir and Hermon,
From the lions' dens,
From the mountains of the leopards.

Thou hast ravished my heart, my sister, my
    bride;

Thou hast ravished my heart with one of
    thine eyes,
With one chain of thy neck.
How fair is thy love, my sister, my bride!
How much better is thy love than wine!
And the smell of thine ointments than all
    spices!
Thy lips, O my bride, drop as the honey-
    comb.
Honey and milk are under thy tongue;
And the smell of thy garments is like the
    smell of Lebanon.

A garden inclosed is my sister, my bride,
A spring shut up, a fountain sealed.
Thy shoots are an orchard of pomegranates,
    with pleasant fruits;
Camphire, with spikenard,
Spikenard and saffron,
Calamus and cinnamon, with all trees of
    frankincense;

Myrrh and aloes, with all the chief spices:
Thou art a fountain of gardens,
A well of living waters,
And streams from Lebanon.

Sonnets from the Portuguese, 14

If thou must love me, let it be for naught
Except for love's sake only. Do not say,
"I love her for her smile—her look—her way
Of speaking gently—for a trick of thought
That falls in well with mine, and certes
    brought
A sense of pleasant ease on such a day"—
For these things in themselves, Belov'd, may
Be changed, or change for thee—and love, so
    wrought,
May be unwrought so. Neither love me for
Thine own dear pity's wiping my cheeks
    dry—
A creature might forget to weep, who bore
Thy comfort long, and lose thy love thereby!
But love me for love's sake, that evermore
Thou may'st love on, through love's eternity.

ELIZABETH BARRETT BROWNING

Poem 94

being to timelessness as it's to time,
love did no more begin than love will end;
where nothing is to breathe to stroll to swim
love is the air the ocean and the land

(do lovers suffer? all divinities
proudly descending put on deathful flesh:
are lovers glad? only their smallest joy's
a universe emerging from a wish)

love is the voice under all silences,
the hope which has no opposite in fear;
the strength so strong mere force is feebleness:
the truth more first than sun more last than
    star

—do lovers love? why then to heaven with hell.
Whatever sages say and fools, all's well.

E. E. CUMMINGS

From *The Good Morrow*

And now good morrow to our waking souls
Which watch not one another out of fear;
For love all love of other sights controls,
And makes one little room an everywhere.
Let sea-discoverers to new worlds have gone,
Let maps to other, worlds on worlds have
    shown;
Let us possess one world, each hath one,
    and is one.

My face in thine eye, thine in mine appears,
And true plain hearts do in the faces rest;
Where can we find two better hemispheres
Without sharp north, without declining west?
Whatever dies was not mixed equally;
If our two loves be one, or thou and I
Love so alike that none do slacken, none can die.

JOHN DONNE

Rue des Vents, VIII

Your body's beauty is an air that blows
Out of some garden where the Spring has
    come—
Where never yet has faded any rose
And never any singing bird is dumb.
You are white waterfalls in piney woods
Touched by the freshness of October wind.
You are the slim young silver moon that
    broods
Over a dusk where lovers wander blind.
And how shall these eyes ever have their fill
Of you, alight with loveliness and love—
My starlight water, tremulous or still,
Across which music wakens as you move!
Over the floor laughing and white you
    pass. . . .
I see all April light that ever was.

ARTHUR DAVISON FICKE

This prose selection may also be appropriately read at a Humanist wedding service:

Desiderata

Go placidly amid the noise and haste, and remember what peace there may be in silence. As far as possible without surrender be on good terms with all persons. Speak your truth quietly and clearly; and listen to others, even the dull and ignorant; they too have their story. Avoid loud and aggressive persons, they are vexatious to the spirit. If you compare yourself with others, you may become vain and bitter; for always there will be greater and lesser persons than yourself. Enjoy your achievements as well as your plans.

Keep interested in your own career, however humble; it is a real possession in the changing fortunes of time. Exercise caution in your business affairs; for the world is full of trickery. But let this not blind you to what virtue there is; many persons strive for high ideals; and everywhere life is full of heroism. Be yourself. Especially, do not feign affection. Neither be cynical about love; for in the face of all aridity and disenchantment it is perennial as the grass.

Take kindly the counsel of the years, gracefully surrendering the things of youth. Nurture strength of spirit to shield you in sudden misfortune. But do not distress yourself with imaginings. Many fears are born of fatigue and loneliness. Beyond a wholesome discipline, be gentle with yourself.

You are a child of the universe, no less than the trees and the stars; you have a right to be here. . . . Whatever your labors and aspirations, in the noisy confusion of life keep peace with your soul. With all its sham, drudgery and broken dreams, it is still a beautiful world. Be cheerful. Strive to be happy.

Spouse _____

Spouse _____

Date _____

Wedding Guests

_____

_____

_____

_____

_____

_____

_____

_____

_____

_____

_____

_____

_____

_____

_____

_____

_____

_____

_____